# How News Travels

By Linda Bruce

# Contents

# Introduction

There are many ways to tell people our news.

We can talk to people on the telephone.

We can write a letter and post it.

faxes machine

We can send emails and faxes using telephone lines.

We can hear the news on the radio, or watch it on television.

Newspapers tell people what is happening in the world.

Some people read the news on the Internet.

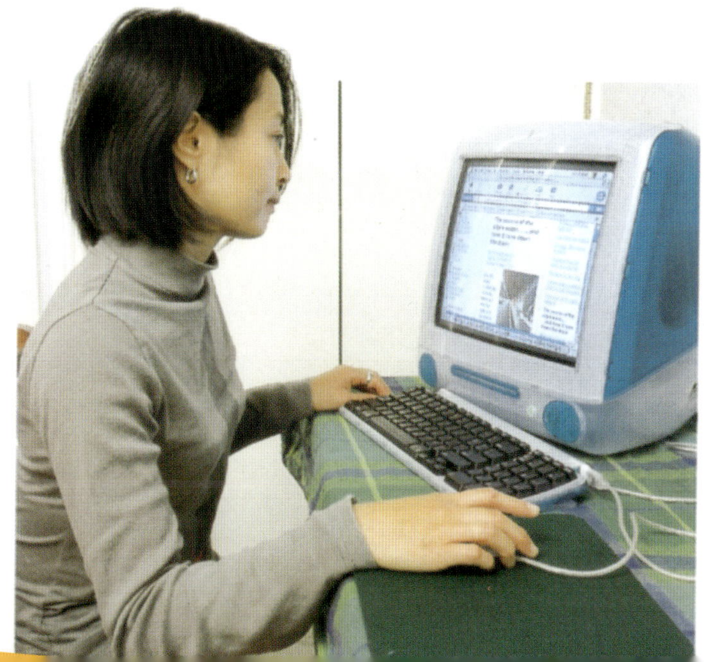

# Talking to people

It is easy to use a telephone to tell friends our news.

We dial our friend's number. After our friend answers the telephone, we talk.

There are many different kinds of telephones.

We can use this kind of telephone anywhere in a house.

Mobile telephones can be used in all kinds of places.

# Writing to people

Another way of telling our news is to send a letter.

First we write the letter.

Then we put it in an envelope.

We address the envelope, and put a stamp on it.

We post the letter in a mail box.

There are different kinds of mail boxes all around the world.

At the mail centre, letters are sorted so that they go to the right places.

Letters are carried between places in vans and trucks.

Ships and planes carry the letters long distances.
It can take days, or even weeks, for long-distance letters to arrive.

Sometimes letters are carried by motorbike.

## Did you know?

The first mail was carried by horse and cart.

# How to send a fax

We can also send a letter using a fax machine. This kind of letter is called a fax.

The boy's letter is made into a signal by this fax machine.

The signal moves along a telephone line to another fax machine.

This fax machine turns the signal back into a letter. Now the girl can read the letter.

## DID YOU KNOW?

People can send pictures, as well as words, in faxes.

## How to send an email

We can send a letter called an email. Email is short for electronic mail.

Emails are sent from computer to computer along the telephone lines.

### Did you know?

Emails can move from one place to another in a few seconds.

Send

The email address goes here.

To: Prue@littlelake.net

Subject: Next Wednesday

What you are writing about goes here.

Hello Prue

Your letter goes here.

Dad says I can come
to your house
after school on Wednesday.
I can't wait to see your new puppy.

From
Anna

Click 'send' to send your email.

# Sending news to many people

People want to know
what is happening all around the world.

They can hear the news on the radio
and on the television.

They can read the news in newspapers, and on the Internet.

## Did you know?

Newspapers are handy because we can read them almost anywhere.

## Listening to the news

People often listen to the news on their radios.

This man is reading the news at a radio station.
His voice is made into radio signals.

Our radios change the signals back into the sound of a voice.

If we have a television,
we can hear and see the news.

Television news moves through the air on radio signals.
The signals carry sound **and** pictures.

# Writing the news down

We have used newspapers for many years to find out the news.

The first newspapers were written by hand. Today, we use computers to write and print newspapers.

The newspapers are carried in trucks to shops.

The news comes on the Internet soon after it has happened.

To use the Internet, we need a computer and a telephone line.

This boy is reading the news on his computer.

## How to make a class newspaper

1. Give your group's newspaper a name.
2. Write the stories, and draw some pictures to go with them.

3. Glue the stories and pictures into the newspaper.

4. Read another group's newspaper.

There are many ways that news travels.
We can find out
what is happening around us
and around the rest of the world.

## Questions

1. How was mail carried at first?
2. What can you send in a fax?
3. How long does it take an email to move from one place to another?
4. Why are newspapers handy?

## Glossary

| | |
|---|---|
| *dial* | to put someone's telephone number into a telephone |
| *email* | a letter sent between computers, using telephone lines |
| *fax* | a letter sent by fax machine, using telephone lines |
| *Internet* | a network of computers that people can use to send or find information |
| *radio signals* | a way of sending sound and pictures through the air |